I0803788

IMAGES
of America

WEST YELLOWSTONE

ON THE COVER: In this undated photograph, the Eagles, one of the town's founding families, get ready for a winter outing. They are standing at the corner of Yellowstone Avenue and Canyon Street, today a busy corner near the entrance to Yellowstone National Park. Winter in West Yellowstone is the main season, with up to six months of snow. Most visitors to West Yellowstone see it in the summer months only. (Yellowstone Historic Center.)

IMAGES
of America

WEST YELLOWSTONE

Paul Shea

ARCADIA
PUBLISHING

Copyright © 2009 by Paul Shea
ISBN 978-0-7385-7087-7

Published by Arcadia Publishing
Charleston, South Carolina

Printed in the United States of America

Library of Congress Control Number: 2009924697

For all general information contact Arcadia Publishing at:
Telephone 843-853-2070
Fax 843-853-0044
E-mail sales@arcadiapublishing.com
For customer service and orders:
Toll-Free 1-888-313-2665

Visit us on the Internet at www.arcadiapublishing.com

This book is dedicated to all the small museums of America, who represent the core of our nation's collective heritage.

Contents

ACKNOWLEDGMENTS

Thanks to Jan Dunbar and Betsy Watry, who deserve writers' credit, for certainly without their help I would not have been able to complete this book. Errors that may have made it into this book are my responsibility alone.

Thanks to my good friend Lee Whittlesey, Yellowstone National Park historian, who introduced me to the history of Yellowstone and the surrounding area, as well as to the joys of interpretation; Thornton Waite, who taught me all I know about the rail operations to and from West Yellowstone; and Jennifer Cantu and Carol Leasure of the Yellowstone Historic Center and volunteer Molly Kline for putting up with all my requests for rescanning of photographs and other needed information. Unless otherwise designated, all photographs used in this volume are from the archives of the Yellowstone Historic Center.

Thanks to the people of the Town of West Yellowstone, who have generously supported the collection, preservation, and interpretation of their history through the efforts of the West Yellowstone Historical Society and the Yellowstone Historic Center. And to all the others, too many to name or remember, whose friendships helped in my understanding of the area history, thank you.

And last but not least, thanks to my good friend Roger, who provided the quiet space I needed to complete this project.

—Paul Shea
March 2009

INTRODUCTION

Situated approximately 3 miles from the Madison River is the gateway town of West Yellowstone, Montana. Located on the west boundary of Yellowstone National Park, it has served millions of visitors to the park for more than 100 years. The arrival of the Union Pacific Railroad's subsidiary, the Oregon Short Line Railroad, in 1908 marks the birth of West Yellowstone.

The west entrance to Yellowstone National Park has a much older history than the town. For more than 8,000 years, humans have used the Madison River as a way to and from the Yellowstone Plateau. Native Americans, early European fur trappers, mining prospectors, scientific surveys, and some of the first stagecoach tours have all used this natural highway to the Yellowstone region.

The basin in which the town is situated is crossed by several primitive Native American trails, one of which is known today as the Bannock Indian Trail. The Bannock/Shoshone Indians are just two of the more than 25 Native American tribes that have a cultural affiliation with the Yellowstone Plateau. Their early system of trails form part of today's highway system that serves Yellowstone National Park.

These trails became more formalized by European visitors and early explorers conducting expeditions on horseback. Soon after the creation of Yellowstone National Park in 1872, roads to accommodate wagons and stagecoaches were developed. A route following the Madison River and another accessing the plateau to the Geyser Basins of the Firehole River were the earliest roads constructed from the west. By 1880, the road up the Madison River from Virginia City, Montana, to Yellowstone National Park was well established, as was a route from eastern Idaho. The Bassett Brother Stage Lines and the Gilmore and Salisbury Stage Line operated both stage and mail routes from eastern Idaho to Mammoth Hot Springs, Yellowstone's north entrance. The Marshall and Goff Stage Line, operating out of Montana, has been credited by many Western historians for initiating the first stagecoach tours of Yellowstone.

In 1897, a new stage road was cut through the forest from the southwest side of the basin to the Madison River just inside the parks' west boundary. This road, which eliminated the older and longer looping Madison River route, was used the following year by the newly formed Monida/Yellowstone Stage Line. In 1898, the Union Pacific Railroad (UPRR) arrived at the border of eastern Idaho and western Montana, where it established a stage and mail stop. This railroad stop, aptly named Monida, a name that represented both states, was a mere 72 miles, or a one-day ride, from the west boundary of Yellowstone National Park. Partnering with Frank J. Haynes, the official Yellowstone National Park photographer, to operate stagecoach tours to the park, the UPRR thus began its long involvement with Yellowstone tourism.

For passengers of the Monida/Yellowstone Stage Line, the first night of the trip was spent at Dwelles' Grayling Inn, located about 8 miles west of present-day West Yellowstone. No longer in existence, Dwelles' was the first commercial establishment in the basin. It hosted as many as 125 visitors per evening through the summer of 1906. In 1905, E. H. Harriman of the UPRR made a personal visit to Yellowstone National Park and ordered the extension of the line from

Ashton, Idaho, to the west boundary of the park. This line was completed in late 1907, and the first passenger train arrived on June 11, 1908.

With the arrival of the train terminus at the west boundary, a town soon arose. Three families acquired forest service leases along the north side of the rail line and opened businesses. Soon after these pioneers began operations, hotels appeared, and subsequently more and more businesses were established. By 1913, there were 13 leaseholders and nearly 50 buildings. At this time, legal proceedings were started to remove the town site from the national forest. In 1920, legislation was passed and signed by Pres. Woodrow Wilson. But it would take until 1924 to completely survey the new town site, which had expanded considerably from its original four blocks. Leaseholders were allowed to buy outright the properties that they had been leasing, and the remaining lots were sold at public auction.

Over the years, the town, whose name changed from Riverside to Yellowstone and finally to West Yellowstone, grew with increased visitation to Yellowstone National Park. In 1916, automobiles were allowed into the park for the first time, and there was a corresponding increase in visitation. Travelers arriving by train and now by personal vehicles expanded the need for increased visitor services. More and more cabin camps were built, and the attending service stations, restaurants, and gift shops grew in numbers as well. Because initially the park was only open during the summer, West Yellowstone was a one-season town, with most of the residents leaving for the winter. However, in 1971, Yellowstone National Park officially opened for the winter, bringing another season of business to West Yellowstone.

Today the town thrives on a busy four-month summer season and a much smaller winter season of over-the-snow travel to the interior of the park. The train is long gone, with passenger service to West Yellowstone ending in 1960. Still the most heavily used entrance of the five that serve Yellowstone National Park, West Yellowstone provides services to more than 1.2 million visitors that travel through the town on their way to the park. The Oregon Short Line Terminus Historic District in West Yellowstone stands today as a showpiece of an era of railroad journeys to our nation's national parks. It is a place where people can marvel at the wonderful architecture left behind by the Union Pacific Railroad and experience the bygone days of train travel.

One

Horses and Stagecoaches

Since the creation of Yellowstone National Park in 1872, visitors used early horse trails and later wagon roads along the Madison River as a route to the park. This rare glass-plate negative of a shepherd's wagon on the west entrance stagecoach road reveals one of the many types of horse-drawn vehicles used to visit Yellowstone. Shepherd wagons were often used as recreational vehicles to tour the park.

Yellowstone Park photographer Frank J. Haynes partnered with the Union Pacific Railroad and established the Monida/Yellowstone Stage Line in 1898 to transport passengers bound for Yellowstone from Monida, Montana. This image depicts a typical 11-passenger coach used by both the Monida/Yellowstone Stage Line and the Yellowstone Park Transportation Company. Manufactured by Abbot and Downing Company, makers of the famous Overland Stagecoach, these touring coaches were made specifically for use in Yellowstone.

Yellowstone Park Transportation coaches such as this one operated out of Mammoth Hot Springs near the north entrance of Yellowstone. Their coaches were painted bright yellow and identified by number. The Yellowstone Park Transportation Company operated transportation by stagecoach until 1917, when the touring operation became motorized and visitors were thereafter transported by touring buses.

The driver of this matched white team was Wilmer Cadmus Greene. Greene hailed from the Ashton, Idaho, area, 57 miles south of the west entrance to Yellowstone. The Monida/Yellowstone Stage Line hired most of its drivers from eastern Idaho and thus provided needed summer employment. Because his drivers acted as early interpreters of the wonders of Yellowstone, owner F. J. Haynes demanded his drivers be articulate and well mannered.

This was one of three Monida/Yellowstone coaches called the Mount Washburn Special. On a typical tour of Yellowstone, an entire day was scheduled for the canyon, which included a half-day tour to the top of Mount Washburn. The coaches seated only five to seven passengers due to the steep climb up the mountain. A five-passenger Mount Washburn coach is on display at the museum in West Yellowstone.

Wilmer Cadmus Greene drove this eight-passenger Yellowstone touring coach from the Monida/Yellowstone Stage Line as he escorted travelers through the wonders of Yellowstone and answered their questions. Although rudimentary in scope, the drivers took time to learn what information was available at the time. Even though humor played a big part in their stories, the stagecoach drivers were considered among the first serious interpreters of Yellowstone National Park.

This image depicts another known Monida/Yellowstone driver, Dave Fuller, with an 11-passenger coach. He married and settled down as a rancher after the era of stagecoaches in Yellowstone ended. His family still lives in the area. From the park's earliest days, scores of people have come to Yellowstone to work seasonally. Many workers, such as Fuller, became attached to the area and eventually made West Yellowstone home.

Charles Rote, another local member of a homesteading family, is captured here driving a five-passenger surrey. These coaches were available for hire if one did not want to ride on the larger coaches. Both the Monida/Yellowstone and Yellowstone Park Transportation Company provided these surreys for hire. During the busy season, these two companies alone operated more than 300 touring coaches.

This undated photograph, one of the earliest taken in the basin, shows the Patt homestead located on Red Creek, now under the waters of Hebgen Lake. Billy Patt worked in Yellowstone National Park for George Marshall, helping to build Marshall's hotel. Patt and his wife, Emma, settled here in 1889, staying until 1898, when they sold to Emma's brother Peter Kerzenmacher and moved to Idaho.

Here is a photograph of the Grayling Post Office, the first in the basin, and postmaster Lulu Kerzenmacher. Lulu was married to Peter Kerzenmacher, brother of Emma Patt. Because the waters of Hebgen Lake would eventually cover their property, they moved their entire homestead to a new location. Here they raised their family, and Peter acted as rancher and hunting guide for many years.

Harry and Sarah Dwelle celebrated their wedding day with this portrait. Harry settled in the Madison Basin near the west entrance to Yellowstone National Park in the mid-1880s. Harry and Sarah built Dwelles' Grayling Inn in 1890 and began offering overnight accommodations to park-bound travelers. In 1898, Dwelle partnered with Frank J. Haynes to provide overnight accommodations for Haynes's Monida/Yellowstone passengers en route to Yellowstone.

Dwelles' Grayling Inn was the first commercial tourist service operation in the Madison Basin. Harry Dwelle was quick to realize the profit that could be gained by providing such services. With his hotel occupancy expectations secured by his 1898 partnership agreement with Haynes and the Monida/Yellowstone Stage Line, Dwelle expanded his operation by adding two more hotel buildings, a saloon, and other structures to serve the booming Yellowstone Park tourist trade.

This view shows some of the enlargement of Dwelles'—several tent buildings that were erected for the 1898 and 1899 seasons and the new buildings that were being erected for support of the tourist trade arriving by the Monida/Yellowstone Stage Line from Monida, Montana. A new house being finished for Walter Wheeler, a friend of Dwelle, is visible just to the right of the tent in this photograph.

Joseph Stimson, a professional photographer from Cheyenne, Wyoming, took this striking photograph. Stimson was touring Yellowstone in either 1905 or 1906 when he captured this scene. Here two Monida/Yellowstone coaches, one leaving and one loading up, prepare to start the second day of the journey from Monida to Yellowstone. By this time, Dwelles' was hosting 150 to 200 tourists each evening. (Wyoming State Archives.)

All Monida/Yellowstone transportation operations were moved to a new site inside the park boundary, as shown in this Frank J. Haynes image, and the barns at Monida, Montana, were abandoned. This new station had every thing necessary for large stagecoach operations in Yellowstone—barns for horses and coaches, paint shops, blacksmith shops, and living quarters for the staff. (Meryl G. Burlingame Special Collections, Montana State University.)

With the completion of the rail line from Ashton, Idaho, to the west boundary of Yellowstone National Park in late 1907, the overnight stop at Dwelles' was no longer needed. Frank J. Haynes sought and received permission to build a facility about a mile inside the park boundary near the west entrance. Pictured here is one of the Monida/Yellowstone coaches at the new location some time between 1908 and 1916.

With visitation increasing every year to Yellowstone National Park, the infrastructure needed to maintain the stage operations led to the economic development of the nearby west entrance. Long winters precluded year-round stock raising or farming. Money was made during the summer months by growing hay for the thousands of horses used in the park and then transporting it in hay wagons, such as this one on the Murray Ranch west of town.

An unidentified photographer took this image of a Monida/Yellowstone stage returning from the park and secured this early view of what is now Yellowstone Avenue, then called Park Street. A typical tour ended in the afternoon and allowed ample time for passengers to dust off and prepare for one last dinner in the nearby Union Pacific restaurant. A 7:30 p.m. train departure signaled a final good-bye to "America's Wonderland."

Two

TRACKS INTO TOWN

A train makes its way up the Warm River Grade from Ashton, Idaho. E. H. Harriman of the Union Pacific Railroad had made a visit to Yellowstone National Park in 1905 with Frank J. Haynes as his guide. During his visit, he made the decision to extend the Union Pacific line from Ashton to the west boundary of Yellowstone National Park. The route had already been surveyed, and work began immediately on the extension.

The "High Bridge," located north of Reas Pass, was similar to high trestles found throughout the American west and was eventually filled in with dirt for two reasons: maintenance costs and fear of fire from the steam engines. Located on the Continental Divide, Reas Pass is the boundary between Montana and Idaho, south of Targhee Pass, over which U.S. 20 crosses the divide.

The line was completed in November 1907, and passenger service began June 11, 1908. In 1909, construction was begun on a depot for the new facility, completed that year and in operation by 1910. The building is made of native rhyolite, volcanic rock from the Yellowstone Caldera eruptions quarried between the west boundary of Yellowstone and Ashton, Idaho.

This early, pre-1922 photograph shows the newly completed depot at the Yellowstone National Park terminus. It was built to show off the first-class service that was paramount to the Union Pacific Railroad. Visible are the beautiful arch windows that give the building its Richardsonian architectural style. In 1922, the porch was expanded and a roof put over it, partially obscuring the windows.

This view of the track side of the new depot shows the two entrances under imposing arch windows. It was here that the visitor could make last-minute changes and arrangements before starting the trip to Yellowstone National Park. The light pink coloring of the stone is still evident today on what is probably the oldest building in West Yellowstone.

This early photograph shows the west end of the depot, a train on the track, and two existing tracks in place. Over time, the increase in visitation to the west entrance would necessitate the building of five sets of tracks. Because there was no space for a roundhouse or turn-around area, a wye was used.

A closer view of the new depot shows the trees that still bordered the track. At left, a man is hosing down the sidewalk. This attention to groundskeeping would result in lawns and sidewalks used to enhance the look of the rail complex. Over the next 20 years, the property would develop a parklike look that is still evident today.

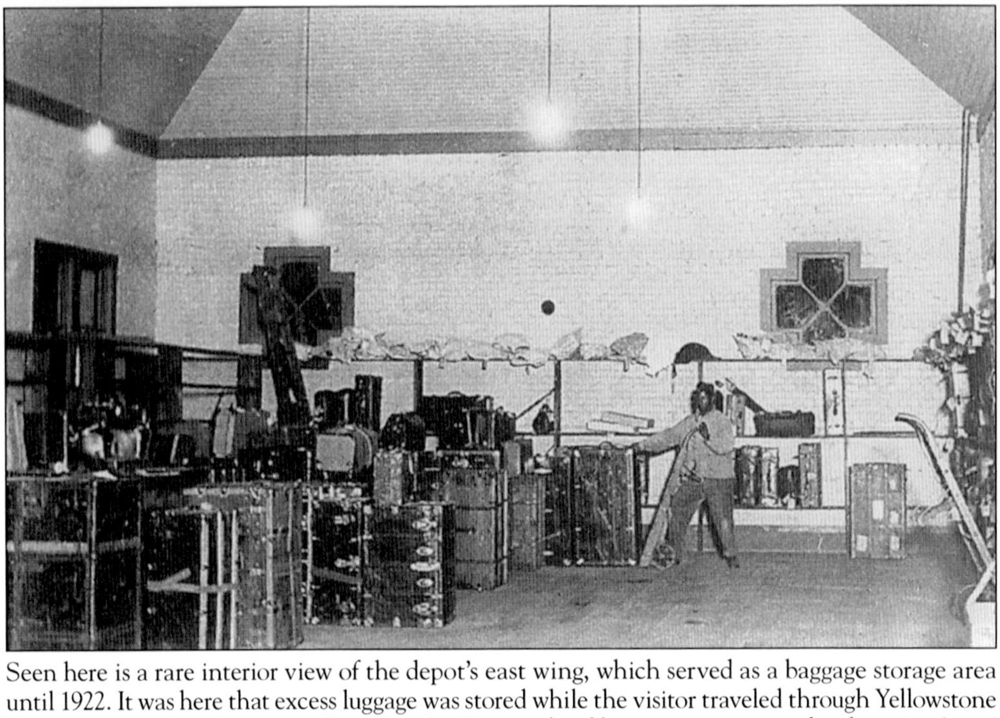

Seen here is a rare interior view of the depot's east wing, which served as a baggage storage area until 1922. It was here that excess luggage was stored while the visitor traveled through Yellowstone National Park. Tourists were allowed only 20 pounds of luggage per person for the trip. At an extra cost, one could have their baggage sent into the park on a separate wagon.

No picture has been found of the first dining room, built in 1908. This is a photograph of the 1911 replacement dining room, called the Beanery. The OSL on the sign stood for the Oregon Short Line Railroad, a subsidiary of Union Pacific. The facilities used that name until 1922, when "Union Pacific" was adopted.

This view of the women's waiting room was taken in 1922, the year that saw extensive enlargement of the rail complex to provide for increased use. Due to the need for showers and changing areas in the depot, the men and women were segregated. "Maids" or attendants assisted the women, and a porter assisted the men. Shoeshine stands were placed in the main lobby.

The ticket window, shown here in 1922, was a center of activity in the town. Here the tourist could make changes to his rail itinerary and locals could buy tickets for their travel needs. As people from other states acquired summer homes in the area, the train was a convenient way to travel back and forth. One could also send and receive Western Union telegraph messages from here.

The newly completed baggage building is shown here, shortly after its construction in 1922. Visitation to Yellowstone experienced one of its periodic growth periods after World War I. The numbers of visitors using the west entrance swelled to as many as 300 to 400 travelers daily. Demand led to the need for a larger baggage facility to hold the excess luggage stored for travelers on tour.

The generator room was under construction in 1910. Electrical power was needed from the beginning, and the distance from existing power sources led Union Pacific to build its own generating plant. It was the first electrical power plant in town and offered extra electricity to the area. This building would be enlarged and generator capacity would increase with the expansion of the rail complex.

The generator room, shown here under construction, matched the rustic architecture of the new depot. This building would undergo additions and modifications in the coming years. Throughout the building era on the rail complex, a style of rustic architecture would emerge. Used for almost all of the buildings here, the rustic architecture mirrored that seen in Yellowstone National Park itself.

With the generator room in the background, the U.S. flag is raised over the new expanse of open ground. The trees had been removed between the generator room and the tracks to allow for a pleasant open park between the depot and dining room. The fences went up to keep local cows from grazing on the new lawns.

Here, in 1918, the generator room is undergoing the first of many additions and expansions. The wood structure was added and a larger three-piston Mercedes Benz diesel generator replaced the original gas generator that had served since 1910. It would serve not only the rail yard but as a backup during electrical outages in town.

Electrical operators stand by one of the early electric boards used to control the feeds to the rest of the complex. In 1947, the Fall River Rural Electrical Co-op from Idaho completed a power line to West Yellowstone. An earlier agreement had been made between the Union Pacific and Fall River to use the generator as an emergency backup system for the town.

This building, the Rest Pavilion, was constructed in the expansion of 1922. As a result of increased visitation, the 1911 dining room was no longer large enough to seat all the arriving passengers at once. The depot, over 250 feet away, was too far from the dining room for people to wait there. This large open-sided structure was placed on the long lawn between the two buildings.

Construction began in April 1925 on a new dining lodge, built on the site of the Rest Pavilion and large enough to handle the tourists arriving both morning and evening. It would be rustic, a style now found throughout the western national parks. Rock and wood taken from the local area went into its construction.

Here masons are stacking the rock for the main fireplace of the dining lodge, with all the rock and timber coming from the local area. The local rhyolite rock with its pink tinge ties it to the Yellowstone Caldera, its source. The further use of native pine and fir add to the rustic elements found throughout this building and others seen in Yellowstone National Park.

The new dining lodge was completed in November 1925 and opened for business the following season with a seating capacity of 350 people at a time. It still stands today as one of a national collection of "Rustic Architecture" built for the national parks by the railroads. Yellowstone National Park superintendent Horace Albright called it one of the most beautiful rustic structures built for a national park.

This view of the west end of the dining lodge shows off the magnificent rock fireplace gracing the main dining hall. The size and scope of the dining lodge was meant to convey a sense of awe and wonder to the arriving visitor. It was but a preview of the wonders waiting in Yellowstone National Park.

4519. Interior Dining Lodge, "Union Pacific System," West Yellowstone, Mont.

This picture postcard of the interior of the dining lodge shows the main dining hall and fireplace. The facility was that of a formal dining lodge with waitresses, linen napkins and tablecloths, and the Union Pacific Railroad's own "Harriman Blue" china service. The floor was concrete with alternating large squares of brown and green. A large rug ran the length of the hall.

This fine-detail photograph shows the recently completed main fireplace. It is shaped like an arrowhead, with the inset seating serving as the notches. It is 18 feet to the top of the arch. The three higher niches are part of the construction of the flue and apparently were never used for any other purpose. Also visible is one of the peeled-log chandeliers suspended from the ceiling.

This is a panoramic view in the opposite direction from the main fireplace. Here the rustic structure is apparent, featuring tall south-facing windows and row after row of peeled-log chandeliers. The kitchen is to the left behind the waitress station. Straight ahead are the steps leading up to the cloakroom. If the doors had been open, one could see the smaller fireplace in the waiting room.

This is a picturesque photograph of the 1926 waitress staff. All waitresses working at West Yellowstone were hired resulting from family connections within the Union Pacific system. They were the daughters of vice presidents and other officials and workers. They came from Nebraska and California as well as small towns across Idaho and Utah.

This is the only known picture of the vast kitchen located in the dining lodge, and it shows only about half of the entire kitchen. It had the usual support facilities nearby—a coal room, a scullery (for the china and silverware), walk-in freezers, linen rooms, and the manager's office. There were also a separate bakery, butcher room, and employee dining room.

The 1911 dining room was remodeled, as shown in this photograph, and a facade added to match the look of the new dining lodge next door. Extensive interior work was done to turn the dining room and kitchen areas into dorms for the 40 to 50 girls who worked there every summer. In the next two years, the remaining smaller buildings were remodeled to reflect the same architecture as well.

To the left in this photograph is the dormitory for men built in 1929, the last major building constructed by the Union Pacific at West Yellowstone. It replaced the old railroad construction crew cars and cabins that had lined the south side of the rail complex. It was also designed to match the overall architectural look of the complex.

This contemporary photograph shows the 1910 water tower built to service the steam engines and other water needs for the facilities. It is a 65,000-gallon, 20-foot-tall tank set on a 50-foot tower. The well and pump house, seen at the bottom of the tower, were constructed in 1908. For the first few years, it supplied water to the town until people could construct their own wells.

Engine No. 3137 is at the water tower in 1955. By 1955, diesels elsewhere were beginning to replace the aging fleet of steam engines. But they would continue on the Yellowstone line through its last summer of operation, 1960. The first diesels made their appearance shortly after that summer on the spring track-plowing operations or would be seen on the occasional special trains operating during the 1960s and early 1970s.

Engine No. 3137 later that same day has been turned around and is ready for departure. Visitors are finishing up their dinners and preparing to depart. The train, called the *Yellowstone Special*, arrived at 7:30 in the morning and left at 7:30 in the evening. The *Yellowstone Special* operated every summer from 1908 through the summer of 1960. During the 1920s, an additional train, the *Yellowstone Express*, was added.

A maintenance crew riding on a handcar was photographed in this undated picture in front of the 1911 dining room. As was common in labor pools, men of different nationalities built the Yellowstone Line from Ashton, Idaho. Among others, there were Greeks and Japanese working on the line. One reason they came was to avoid military drafts in their own countries.

This picture of a train crew was taken in the early years of operations at West Yellowstone. From left to right are the fireman, the engineer, the conductor, and two brakemen. The engineer and fireman ran the complicated steam engine used to pull the train. The conductor and brakemen helped with operations and took care of the passengers. There were also the usual black porters aboard as well.

A few years later, as shown in the different cut of the uniforms, this crew of conductor and brakemen were photographed beside the *Yellowstone Special.* The conductor was in control of the entire train. His word was law and the train did not move until he gave the order. He was responsible for the make up of the train and collecting the passengers' tickets once aboard.

Clifford Peake, an electrician, is pictured here with the depot in the background. Clifford helped run the electrical generator and worked at West Yellowstone from 1918 to 1928. His photographs comprise some of the earliest ones taken of the West Yellowstone rail complex. Over the years, the Peake family, of eastern Idaho, would work as conductors, a lawyer, and a host of other railroad jobs on the Yellowstone Line.

An early-1920s dining-lodge crew—waitresses, cooks, busboys, manager, and a bus driver—line up for a group photograph. The girl on the right in the back row wearing a black blouse is a maid. She probably worked in the women's wing of the depot, helping the women with the changing of clothes and other necessities.

The uniforms had changed, but little else had in this late 1950s photograph. The numbers of rail travelers had declined remarkably from the 1920s and 1930s. By 1955, the *Yellowstone Special* was running only three days a week and the dining lodge was open to the public for dinner. Union Pacific still staffed a full complement of workers even though numbers were sometimes less than 50 passengers a day.

This publicity photograph was taken probably in the early 1920s; women were just then starting to wear pants! Here the *Yellowstone Special* is accompanied by a bear, used to promote travel to the nation's first national park. From 1923 through 1960, bears would be the chosen image for the Union Pacific Railroad in a 46-year-long advertising campaign for Yellowstone.

A group of visitors in the early 1900s poses on the back of the *Yellowstone Special*, with one of the party taking a photograph. She is probably using one of the new box cameras that would revolutionize photography and open it up to the common traveler. These photographs of the *Yellowstone Special* became a favorite keepsake of one's trip to Yellowstone.

Three

OPEN FOR BUSINESS

Sam Eagle, left, sits near the Fountain Hotel in Yellowstone National Park. Eagle was one of the first three to apply for a lease at the National Forest Service site located near the terminus of the new rail line. He had been a fishing guide and bartender at the hotel when he met his future wife, Ida Carlson, a waitress. They opened the first general store in the new town.

Pictured at right is the Eagle Store as it appeared about 1913. Located on the corner of Park Street and Second Avenue, now the corner of Canyon Street and Yellowstone Avenue, this would become the main corner of business in town. One block to the right is the entrance to Yellowstone National Park. This photograph was taken from the site now housing the Visitor Information Center.

This view from the depot shows the Eagle Store at center. To the left is Joseph Clause's cabin. Clause located here in 1908 from Henry's Lake, Idaho, on a site near the west of town. To the far right is the site of Charles Arnet's property. Arnet was one of the first three lease holders, later selling his lease to the Stuarts in 1910.

Dick Murray, the third leaseholder of 1908, built the Yellowstone Hotel. It was located across the street from the Eagle Store to the west. It served the traveling public, although the automobiles in this photograph were not allowed into Yellowstone National Park until 1916. From 1908 to 1916, business was quiet in town, with rail passengers making up the majority of visitors.

Here the Yellowstone Hotel has been flanked by a restaurant, dance hall, and pool hall. With the addition in 1916 of automobile travel in Yellowstone National Park, work picked up for the new town businesses. The town started to grow more and more as visitation increased after World War I. Hotels such as the Yellowstone provided for the traveler who did not wish to camp out.

Alex Stuart's General Merchandise store provides a backdrop to a rodeo in this photograph, possibly of a Fourth of July celebration. Alex had come to West Yellowstone as a partner of Sam Eagle. Charles Arnet originally leased this site, but he decided to move his business one block east towards the park and sold his lease to Stuart. When Arnet left town, Stuart would buy that lease as well.

Louis Kennedy, the Madison Basin forest ranger, built the Curio Shop. He had to sell the lease on this property site due to the conflict of interests of a local ranger preempting prime town sites for himself. Later Sam Eagle and Alex Stuart bought the building and lease. The Eagle family would eventually buy out the Stuarts, and the Eagles still operate the store today.

This is a tintype of Roxy Bartlett as a young man. By 1909, Roxy was a stagecoach driver for the Monida/Yellowstone Stage Line. He and his new wife, Dolly, arrived in the spring of 1909 and settled in West Yellowstone. Dolly went to work for one of the early tent hotels, the Madison, located across the street from the depot. They would purchase the facility and lease about 1911.

This photograph, taken in 1919, focuses east along Yellowstone Avenue toward the west entrance to Yellowstone National Park. On the right is the Tepee Inn under construction; it was located across the street from the Madison Hotel. Business was beginning to grow, and the town was expanding to the west along Yellowstone Avenue. As more and more visitors arrived, services were springing up quickly.

This photograph shows the Madison Hotel a few years after its construction. Roxy and Dolly Bartlett had replaced the old tent camp with a six-room log hotel. Business was picking up, and the Madison was one of the better hotels in town. Over the years, it has hosted movie stars and Pres. Herbert Hoover on his fly-fishing trips to the area. It is still in business today.

This undated photograph of the interior of the Madison Hotel features the rustic furnishings found in lodges throughout the area. Bearskin rugs, antlers on the walls, and wicker furniture were common elements. The Madison had a rock-and-cement fireplace, log walls, and drinking fountains made from large log burls. The drinking fountains are still in the lobby.

A brochure for one of the small camping companies that operated throughout Yellowstone National Park, the R. C. Bryant Company, offered two trips a season to the park. Tourists could travel to West Yellowstone by train and then spend a night in the Bryant Way Hotel, located on Park Street. A second night could be spent before departure.

This is one of the few photographs of the Bryant Way Hotel, at left, in West Yellowstone. Bryant sold the hotel several years after it was built. It would remain in service until about 1920, when it was razed. The large building in the center is Alex Stuart's garage, and his home on the far right.

This is one of the only photographs showing passengers embarking at the depot, taken in 1915. It was here that tourists would begin their journey to Wonderland. "Ho for the park" was heard as the coaches moved out on their way for a five-day loop through Yellowstone. This narrow loading platform would be made larger in the 1922 expansion of the rail property.

Monida/Yellowstone stagecoaches head out at the newly constructed depot. The bright red coaches of the M/Y added color to the tours through Yellowstone National Park. The bright yellow of the Yellowstone Park Transportation Company coaches, other private wagons, and camping coaches all would have been quite the sight to see as one circled the park.

167. Oregon Short Line Depot, Yellowstone National Park

Here is a fine view of the porte cochere and stages loaded for a trip to Yellowstone. Tours would depart from here for what was commonly a five-day tour. Travelers spent nights in the magnificent hotels built by the Northern Pacific Railroad throughout the tour. Old Faithful Inn, Lake Hotel, Canyon Hotel, and the Mammoth Hot Springs Hotel would provide the kind of service the seasoned traveler expected and demanded.

Four

The Town Grows and Changes

Here is the Eagle store about 1920. With the introduction of the automobile in 1916 and the end of World War I, things were picking up, and the store had expanded. Two of the autos seen here are loaded with camping gear. The first auto-camp in Yellowstone National Park was located just 14 miles inside the west entrance at Madison Junction.

Unfortunately unfocused, this is one of the only photographs of the interior of the new Eagle Store and Post Office built in the mid-1920s. Sam Eagle was postmaster at West Yellowstone from 1909 until 1935. In 1908, a post office was established with the name "Riverside." In 1909, the name was changed to "Yellowstone," and in 1920, the "West" was added.

Pictured here is the new Eagle Store, built between 1927 and 1930. The town and the Eagles had prospered during the first 20 years of existence. With the removal of the town site from the Madison National Forest (latter renamed the Gallatin National Forest), properties were purchased by the lease holders, which allowed for better financial stability. Until 1920, all property was leased from the government on a year-to-year basis.

Another undated photograph shows the growth north along Canyon Street. The pool hall would change hands over time and serve a variety of functions, including that of a bakery. The large building to the right is the Yellowstone Hotel, which moved to this location from its place on Yellowstone Avenue during one of West Yellowstone's remodels. It was moved again in the 1940s.

In a photograph taken shortly after it was built, the Tepee Inn reflects the rustic style used in early construction around West Yellowstone. Efforts to match the look of the railroad property and buildings in Yellowstone National Park were reflected in the local architecture. At one point, the National Park Service offered its architect to help plan the town. However, locals turned down this generous offer.

Cars, shown here in an early-1920s photograph of the Tepee Inn, would come to dominate the visitation to Yellowstone National Park. From the inception of the park in 1872, the horse and coach was the main mode of transportation. In 1916, the automobile was allowed in Yellowstone, long after the rest of the nation had turned to its use.

The Madison Hotel, here in the early 1920s, was growing to fill the demand of increased visitation after World War I. A large addition was attached to the original six rooms, and indoor plumbing was added at this point, too. The Madison would remain one of the finer hotels in town until the late 1940s.

This photograph shows an expanded Madison Hotel to which a small dance hall had been added on the west side. A new wing of rooms was added to the rear of the original structure, bringing the room total to 22. The cabins in the back were houses for the Bartletts, and more would be added. These cabins would eventually be replaced with a modern motel.

This photograph of the depot before the 1922 alterations was taken from the Eagle Store porch. Although town businesses would profit more from the auto trade than rail passengers, it was the promotional efforts of the Union Pacific Railroad that led to the west entrance of Yellowstone National Park becoming the busiest entrance in 1913, a distinction that it still holds today.

This photograph, taken in the 1920s, shows the Smith and Chandler building, which stands where the Stuart store once was. Here a crowd surrounds a tepee and family from the Bannock/ Shoshone Reservation at Blackfoot, Idaho. The Native Americans sold jewelry and posed for photographs for the tourists, who were always looking for a Wild West experience.

An undated photograph shows the first school in West Yellowstone. By 1913, there was a need for schools in the basin. Three schools were built that year—one in West Yellowstone, one 8 miles west of town, and one on the north side of Hebgen Lake. Over the years, consolidation would lead to the closing of the two basin schools and place all school services in town.

School kids and their teacher line up in this undated photograph of the school in West Yellowstone. In 1913, when the school opened, the townspeople enrolled two underage children in order to have enough students to qualify for state funding. The school was built to a standard set of plans provided by the State of Montana. This school would be replaced by a larger one in 1918.

Schoolteacher Jessie Donaldson is out for a day skiing. Jessie taught for only two years in West Yellowstone before moving on, but she was among the first teachers in the basin. Later Jessie married James Willard Schultz, noted western author of *My Life as an Indian* and *Blackfeet Tales of Glacier National Park*. Jessie acted as photographer for Schultz on his trips throughout the Glacier Park area.

This photograph shows the 1918 school and additions. The rock facing on the entrance was not a standard feature of Montana schools; a part of the facing fell off during the 1959 Hebgen Lake earthquake. This school sits on the site of the 1913 school. The earlier school was moved across the street, where it serves as a business today. A high school was added in 1964.

By the late 1930s, West Yellowstone had been expanding north, as this photograph along Canyon Street between Yellowstone and Madison Avenues shows. Cafés and bars were big business there during Prohibition and the Depression. Doc's was one of the favorites, featuring nightly dancing to swing and jazz bands. The large building on the corner to the right was the Rustic Theater.

This is Walt Stuart's garage. Walt's father, Alex, was one of the early settlers in West Yellowstone. This Texaco station sat across the street from the Eagle Store on the site of the Murray's Yellowstone Hotel complex, at the corner of Canyon Street and Yellowstone Avenue. The Murrays had sold out but retained their homestead west of town. Walt would operate this service station for many years until it was destroyed by fire in the 1970s.

Shown here is Lorey's, one of the early service stations in West Yellowstone. Built in the rustic architecture style, it was situated on the north side of the Eagle property, which can be seen here on the right side of the photograph. The Eagles eventually bought out Lorey's and now run a newer service station on the site.

Mechanics line up at Alex Stuart's garage at the west entrance. In the days when automobiles required a lot of work to keep running, these mechanics and entrepreneurs were kept busy during the summer season. Originally there were several blacksmith shops in West Yellowstone, but they were eventually replaced by service stations. Automobiles greatly changed the nature of travel to the park.

The Whitman brothers' garage, shown here in an undated photograph, is located on the corner of U.S. 20 and U.S. 191 (Canyon Street). The Whitmans had been in the area since the late 1880s, first at Henry's Lake in Idaho and eventually settling in the West Yellowstone area. The station has been rebuilt and added on to over the years but is still in service today under new ownership.

Another rustic structure was the Totem on Canyon Street, two blocks north of Yellowstone Avenue. By the late 1940s, the Totem was a fixture on Canyon Street. To the right of the Totem one can see the corner of the Visitor's Bureau Gift Shop. Cinder-block construction was replacing the log structures of earlier years.

This 1950s photograph of the Big Chief Motel shows a typical motor inn of the day. These motels started as cabin camps with little or no amenities, usually just a couple of beds in a cabin. They met the growing demand for better services by adding bedding, indoor plumbing, and maid service. By the 1950s, West Yellowstone was housing many small motels serving the auto trade.

The Stage Coach Inn is pictured shortly after its construction in 1948. Visitors wanted better accommodations, and this inn met the needs. It surpassed the older hotels, such as the Madison, for style and service. In the coming years, the hotel would replace the motel as the traveler's choice for overnight accommodations. The Stage Coach Inn has a sister hotel in Jackson, Wyoming, the Wort. The Stage Coach Inn is still in operation today.

An undated photograph shows the Rainbow Tabernacle. It was built to cater to the needs of those seeking spiritual guidance. Stories recount elder A. C. Stubbs waiting outside the many bars found in West Yellowstone as patrons headed home late in the evening, encouraging them to seek redemption. The tabernacle passed into history and today has been replaced by a warehouse.

This photograph shows the town on a busy summer day in the 1940s. During World War II, rail traffic was suspended, and for three years, the town's businesses struggled with reduced visitation due to gas and tire rationing. In Yellowstone, only the camps were open, the hotels having been closed for the duration of the war. Only those tourists nearest Yellowstone National Park could make the trip for a visit.

This nice, 1950s view is looking east down Madison Avenue to the corner of Madison and Canyon Street. On the left are the Pine Cone Cabins, one of the many cabin camps found around town. These would be replaced by motels and today's hotels and suites. The West Yellowstone Bakery on the right is located where the Rustic Theater was before it burned down in 1941.

Another 1950s photograph, taken from the corner of Madison Avenue and Canyon Street, is looking south down Canyon Street. From the Cowboy Bar and down the street to the left is the block that was rebuilt after the 1941 fire. The number of cars shows the busy summer season in West Yellowstone. At this time, the streets were sparsely paved. Note the water in the intersection. Streets were dramatically improved in 1988.

An image of Union Pacific letterhead for West Yellowstone shows the touring buses that replaced the stagecoaches in 1916. Throughout the 1920s, the Union Pacific would expand the rail complex and see more and more visitors arriving at West Yellowstone. Partly due to Union Pacific's promotions of Yellowstone National Park, the west entrance became the busiest entrance of the five that serve Yellowstone.

When this picture was taken in 1922, the use of trains to travel to Yellowstone National Park was in its heyday, lasting until World War II. A fleet of 200-plus bright yellow buses picked up visitors at one of four gateway towns around the park. The former five-day tour of the stagecoach era was already gone, reduced to only three days.

In the late 1930s, around the time this photograph was taken, the number of visitors arriving by train was already declining. More and more travelers were using their own automobiles for vacations. Those arriving by train did not carry any less luggage than before. The limit of 20 pounds per person, in effect during the stagecoach days, still held. Just like carry-on luggage today, the suitcases appeared to fit a standard size.

A late 1920s photograph shows the White Motor Coach buses lined up for Yellowstone Park tours. By 1926, there were approximately 250 buses in the Yellowstone fleet. They picked up passengers from West Yellowstone, Gardiner, and Red Lodge, Montana. For a short period in the 1920s, these buses were being used for tours originating in Lander, Wyoming, some 200 miles south of the park.

EATING HOUSE - WEST YELLOWSTONE

Pictured here is architect Gilbert Stanley Underwood's design of the new dining lodge at West Yellowstone. To accommodate the increase in visitation in the 1920s, Union Pacific had expanded its services at West Yellowstone. Underwood would design not only this building for the Union Pacific but virtually all the buildings in the Southern Utah National Parks for the National Park Service as well. His architectural signature also adorns many other park and public buildings.

The Union Pacific dining lodge, shown here in a photograph taken in the 1950s, was a monumental structure in keeping with the idea of "park architecture." At West Yellowstone, the dining lodge and depot were designed to provide first-class service as well as to introduce the grandeur of the nearby national park. Robert Reamer introduced this architectural style in the early 1900s at Old Faithful Inn.

In this photograph, taken in 1947, the slow decline of rail travel was apparent, but one would still be met by the waitresses with song outside the dining lodge upon arrival. First-class travel was still the railroad way. From the Pullman cars to the dining cars to the facilities that awaited visitors at West Yellowstone, train travel was a special experience.

This undated photograph shows the West Yellowstone Union Pacific terminus; here tens of thousands of visitors from all over the world arrived on their way to Yellowstone National Park. Passenger service was stopped after the summer of 1960. Left today is the largest rail complex built to serve a national park. The women's dorm on the left burned down in 1978; the rest of the buildings survive.

This view from the water tower shows most of the completed complex built by the railroad between 1909 and 1929. It was truly a setting cut out of the dense, lodgepole pine forest bordering Yellowstone National Park. Part of the wye is visible at the lower right. Trains were backed down this side and then driven forward on another set of tracks before backing up to the depot.

This view shows the town in 1940; this would be the pause before the storm of autos. Although nobody at this time knew it, World War II was on the way. There would be three years when the trains did not run to West Yellowstone. When they resumed in 1946, the railroad would never again see visitor rail use as high as it was in the 1920s and 1930s.

As seen in this 2007 photograph, the people of West Yellowstone have not forgotten their colorful past. In 1998, work was started on the restoration of the historic district. Grounds were brought back to life and the depot and dining lodge had major restoration completed by the town's centennial in 2008. Today the Yellowstone Historic Center operates a museum in the original depot built in 1909.

Five

Touring Buses and an Airport

A White Motor Coach touring bus on the beginning of a tour to Yellowstone sits in front of the Eagle Store in this early-1920s photograph. One can see why they were known as "open top buses." The canvas roof could be folded back if the weather permitted. The 11 passengers are bundled up on this cold morning, though. Luggage was carried in the canvas boot on the rear.

Another early-1920s photograph shows a White Motor Coach bus with the top up. There were no windows on the buses until 1931. Lap blankets were provided for the passengers, as heaters were not included as part of the buses' makeup. The rollback top was a must for touring the park, where vistas were stunning and required an open view.

Like the stagecoach companies before them, the Yellowstone Park Transportation Company provided smaller touring cars; this one is a Lincoln. They were available, at an extra charge, for shorter trips or for more privacy on the tour. Equipped with jump seats in the back, they could accommodate five passengers.

This photograph, taken before 1922, shows a White Motor Coach bus and drivers at West Yellowstone. Beginning in 1916 and lasting until 1938, White would provide the majority of buses for Yellowstone. These 11-passenger buses where designed to handle the rough, unpaved, mountainous roads found in Yellowstone. They were painted bright yellow, the Yellowstone Park Transportation Company color that had been used since 1883.

This pre-1919 photograph shows some of the White Motor Coach buses getting ready for the morning tour departures. Drivers and buses were stationed just inside the west entrance at the Riverside facility. The two competing stage lines, Monida/Yellowstone and the Yellowstone Park Transportation Company, were consolidated into the Yellowstone Park Transportation Company. Approximately 90 of these buses were in use by 1917.

Another early photograph shows buses lined up on Yellowstone Avenue. Expecting some 400 passengers most days at West Yellowstone, there would be a need for 30 to 40 of the buses every day. In 1938, the last year the buses were manufactured, the Yellowstone fleet was the second-largest public transportation fleet in America, after Greyhound.

This is a photograph of one of the two Model 50 buses produced in 1923. They were much larger than the other models, holding 25 passengers each. They turned out to be a failure for park use. Equipped with a four-cylinder engine, they were underpowered. The two buses, the only ones ever made, were sent to West Yellowstone for use until they were sold during World War II.

This is a 1938 photograph of Yellowstone Park Transportation Company driver Charles Narghang, who drove in Yellowstone National Park for three summers. He left behind a photograph album of his summers driving, a wonderful collection of photographs now in the Yellowstone Historic Center Archives. Later Charles would take up guiding on the Missouri River; it was on one of those trips that he passed away.

This photograph shows Charles Narghang and Bus 437 at the West Yellowstone depot. During this period, a loud voice from Smith and Chandler, a store located across the street, would announce, "Don't forget your bus pictures!" A photographer would approach the bus and take a group photograph, which would be ready for the passengers when they returned to town. Some of these photographs were made into postcards.

Another photograph taken in the 1950s shows the popular practice of group photographs. The driver is Garth Schomler of West Yellowstone. Garth drove school buses in the Los Angeles area during the winter months, then buses at Yellowstone in the summer. He and his wife, Marguerite, eventually settled in West Yellowstone and ran a curio shop until 2007.

An early-1920s photograph shows a large group about to enter Yellowstone Park. The young man in the front seat with a young boy on his lap is Clifford Peake. Peake worked for the Union Pacific Railroad at West Yellowstone from 1918 through 1928 and left behind a collection of some of the earliest pictures taken of the rail property.

This is a mid-1930s photograph of a group about to embark on their tour of Yellowstone Park. Only sunny days permitted touring with the top down and only at the beginning of the tour. Although it was a treat to expose the view in this way, it would eventually become too hot and the leather seats too warm to sit in. The driver is Gene Hungerford of Great Falls, Montana.

This photograph shows Grace Coolidge, wife of Pres. Calvin Coolidge, in one of the Lincoln touring cars. Over the years, several presidents have visited Yellowstone National Park. In early days, they toured Yellowstone in the company buses. In more recent times, the president was taken around in the official presidential car. Herbert Hoover visited several times to fly-fish and stayed at least once in the Madison Hotel.

Feeding the bears by the side of the road became a famous Yellowstone Park tradition, shown here in the 1920s. It was part of the tour and was allowed although park rules forbade it even then. Taking a tour of Yellowstone offered city folk a look at nature they would never see otherwise. Feeding bears was finally prohibited in the late 1960s.

Herklas Rightenour is shown on his tractor clearing stumps for the airport. In 1932, town leaders decided West Yellowstone needed an airport, and they put up $1,000 to get started. With a permit from the Federal and Montana Aviation Commissions, they began construction on a mile-long runway on the west end of town. Service began in 1935, provided by National Park Airways, a subsidiary of Western Airlines.

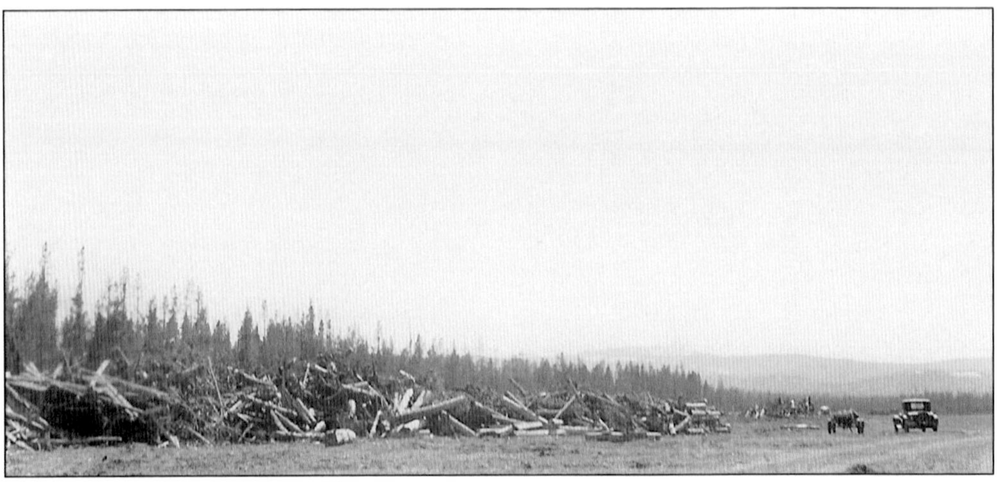

This c. 1934 photograph shows the number of trees cut down to clear the area for a new airport. Operating only during the summer months, the airfield had two runways, a log hangar, and a small building to handle passengers, baggage, and freight. Located on the west side of West Yellowstone, it is now a large open field.

Crowds gather around Chris Christensen's plane on the first day of air service to West Yellowstone. Most of this day was spent taking town folks up for a flight in the seven-passenger Fokker. A second runway was already under construction, and soon a large hangar and other service buildings would be added.

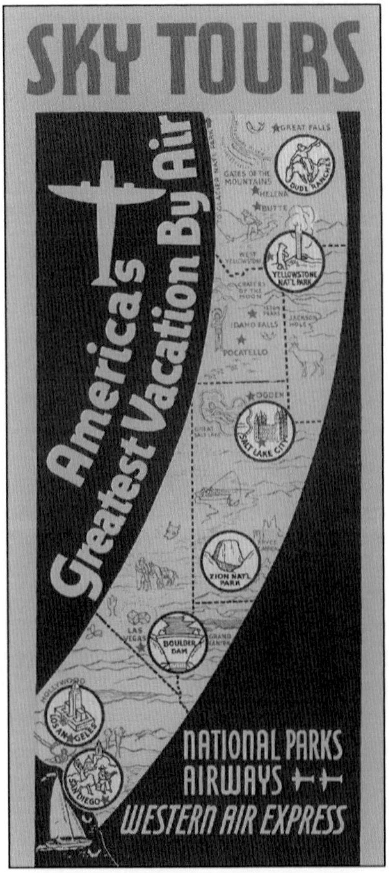

A 1936 brochure for National Park Airways, a subsidiary of Western Airlines, shows the new service to West Yellowstone. As seen here on the cover, they flew to several of the West's tourist areas. It was easy to add West Yellowstone to the schedule, a service that continued on to Great Falls, Montana. This service brought West Yellowstone closer to the traveling public than ever before.

Here a Western Airlines plane is greeted with fanfare and a waiting stagecoach. This Monida/Yellowstone coach was used around West Yellowstone for years; this could be either the first day of the season or a special charter flight. Celebrating the first day opening of the season began when the railroad and stage companies handed out "First Day In" pins and ribbons.

In this undated photograph, crew and aircraft passengers get ready to depart West Yellowstone. Air travel was now supplanting rail travel in America. Western Airlines would provide seasonal air flights to West Yellowstone until 1951. The approach and takeoffs over the town became a problem for the larger airplanes coming into service, and there would be no commercial service again until 1963.

This photograph of the newest airport, located 3 miles north of town, was taken shortly after construction around 1963. Western Airlines had stopped flying into West Yellowstone by 1951. The use of larger planes and takeoffs and landings over the town itself was no longer an option. This expanded facility today serves the traveling public during the summer season with flights from Salt Lake City, Utah.

This photograph, probably taken in the late 1930s or early 1940s, is one of the earliest photographs of West Yellowstone from the air. The railroad property, including the wye turnaround, can be seen on the left side of the town. The town's major growth to this time had been centered on Yellowstone Avenue and Canyon Street.

Six

Earthquake and Fire

This photograph is iconic for Montana, featuring pristine rivers and fly-fishing, a sport popular for many years. On the night of August 17, 1959, this idyllic scene would turn to one of devastation and tragedy. The mountainside at center would collapse in one of America's largest earthquakes, registering 7.5 on the Richter scale. (Montana Highway Department.)

Illustrating the slide, one can see the lighter part from center to lower left corner. At approximately 11:30 on the night of August 17, 1959, the Yellowstone area was shaken awake by this quake. The magnitude of this event shattered rock that was holding up the mountainside and sent it sliding down into the Madison River. (Montana Highway Department.)

Pictured here is another view of the slide. It is estimated that the slide contained between 28 and 33 million cubic meters of material. It created hurricane-force winds in the narrow canyon. The material from the mountain blocked off the Madison River, seen in the center with water backing up behind the slide. (Montana Highway Department.)

This photograph, looking east on the Madison River, shows the new lake forming behind the slide, now known as Earthquake or Quake Lake. Thousands of trees were flooded. Cabins floated off their foundations. The lake today is still full of dead and standing trees. Estimates state that the earth dam will last several hundred years before the river cuts through the slide and empties. (Montana Highway Department.)

Searchers look for bodies of missing campers soon after the quake. A National Forest Service campground was located directly below the slide. Only seven bodies were recovered, and 19 or more are believed to be buried under the slide. Several more died of their injuries in the following days. Two campers were killed west of the quake by falling rocks as well. (Montana Highway Department.)

This photograph shows the hastily built new road put in to bypass sections of road that had dropped into Hebgen Lake, some 5 miles upriver from the slide. Several hundred people were trapped between the slide and Hebgen Dam due to road damage. U.S. Air Force helicopters from around the West were immediately dispatched to help with rescue operations. (Montana Highway Department.)

Within weeks, the U.S. Army Corps of Engineers, shown here, began work to cut a spillway across the slide to let the Madison River flow downstream. During the night of the earthquake, many feared that either the slide or the Hebgen Lake Dam, which had been damaged, would give way, flooding communities downriver. Ennis, Montana, was briefly evacuated that evening. (Montana Highway Department.)

In this view, work is being done on the slide debris on the opposite side of the canyon. It would be leveled to accommodate the Earthquake Visitor Center and memorial to those who died. Thousands of visitors yearly stop to view this slide and learn about its history, as well as information about earthquakes worldwide. (Montana Highway Department.)

This photograph shows the nearly completed spillway already full of water. The work done by the U.S. Army Corps of Engineers stabilized the new lake and put in new highway where needed. The Hebgen Dam was stabilized and damage repaired. Waves formed by the quake had sloshed over the dam and destroyed the old dam spillway. (Montana Highway Department.)

This photograph, near today's Kirkwood Resort, shows road damage and the new shoreline of Hebgen Lake. The north shore of the man-made Hebgen Lake dropped several feet, taking portions of the road with it as well as some houses. Temporary roadways were put into place until new roads could be built. (Montana Highway Department.)

This photograph, looking west above Hebgen Lake Dam, shows the damage to the existing road. Here Hebgen Lake has completely covered the road, making passage impossible. In the hours following the quake, this kind of road damage hindered the rescue efforts for those campers stranded near the slide. (Montana Highway Department.)

Here is road damage near Cougar Creek, just north of West Yellowstone. For days after the quake, only four-wheel-drive vehicles were able to travel north to the slide area. All locals who had such vehicles were pressed into service to help with the evacuation of the quake area. Several roads inside Yellowstone National Park also suffered quake damage. (Montana Highway Department.)

More road damage is shown near Duck Creek, north of West Yellowstone. The driver of this car was staying in a nearby cabin camp and fled south toward West Yellowstone. In the dark, he did not see the road damage and ended up here. He was unhurt in the accident but suffered cuts to his head while climbing through a broken window. (Montana Highway Department.)

This dramatic photograph shows how much the north side of Hebgen Lake dropped during the quake. The road comes from the upper right, where a house is under water, only its roof showing. Divers were sent into the lake around such areas to check for bodies. Fortunately none were found. The cabins and homes had been evacuated safely. (Montana Highway Department.)

This photograph shows damage to the town's pharmacy. Most damage in West Yellowstone consisted of porches and brickwork falling off, broken windows, and downed chimneys. Only slight injuries were reported and no deaths. On the railroad property, all chimneys, including the large dining lodge chimney, came down. There were also 400 broken windows in the railroad buildings.

Here is a view from behind the counter at the town's pharmacy. Damage such as this was common all over town. Most did not think of taking pictures. They were more concerned with the many aftershocks of the main quake and spent their time trying to clean up. Because of all the damage and publicity, the season was over.

The theater goes up in flames along with half of the block in this 1941 photograph. Fires were the bane of all western towns, and West Yellowstone was not spared. Wood buildings, wood-burning stoves, and primitive electrical equipment all added to the possibility of fire. Over the years, several of the town's businesses burned down. The Smith and Chandler store was destroyed in one such fire in the early 1970s.

Another dramatic photograph of the 1941 fire is seen here. Salvaged goods are piled in the street across from the inferno. Stacks of hats and other Western ware attest to the tourist trade. Fires such as this would force some out of business. With a season of just approximately 120 days, losing a summer's worth of business was catastrophic.

The fire burned south to Jeanette's Café and stopped at Doc's Bar. This block would be quickly rebuilt, but the theater would be relocated across Canyon Street. Doc's Bar weathered the fire and would continue business. Doc Bartlett, the owner, was a brother to Roxy Bartlett, builder of the Madison Hotel.

In 1942, the Three Bear Lodge burned to the ground. Fire has always been a problem in western cities because of the log and wood structures. Volunteer fire departments did their best to cope with these periodic fires. In a cruel twist of fate, the replacement structure of Three Bear Lodge would burn down in early 2008.

In the early 1970s, the Smith and Chandler store fell victim to fire. Unlike the fire of 1941, this one was confined to the one store. A volunteer fire department had been formed to deal with such disasters. The Smith and Chandler store was rebuilt, but not as a log building replicating the original. Today a modern fire department defends the town from such fires.

Seven

THE WEST GATE

In 1907, when this postcard was produced, no buildings existed at the west entrance to Yellowstone National Park. The railroad was nearing completion but would not arrive until November 1907. F. J. Haynes's postcard is a composite, a technique he used to remake a photograph to fit the times. No buildings would appear at the west entrance for another year.

By 1918, when this photograph was taken, the west entrance road had been realigned. The original stage road angles off to the left behind the horse, and the auto road is to the right. The horse is tied to the first auto entrance station at the west entrance, automobiles having been allowed in Yellowstone National Park since 1916. Traffic at the west entrance increased each year.

This 1918 photograph shows the first auto entrance station at the west entrance. A mileage sign shows distances to points throughout the park; notices and park regulations were tacked on the front of the building. Tourists could stop to buy an auto pass from National Park Service rangers. The entrance was located exactly at the park boundary. This facility was replaced in 1924.

In 1924, a new gate, shown here, was built to handle the increase in automobile traffic at the west entrance, which had been moved 100 yards inside the park. This move eased the congestion of autos backed up in town on busy mornings. Ultimately two other gates would be constructed and positioned further inside the park. The gate today is approximately a half-mile inside the park.

National Park Service rangers are shown at the west entrance in the 1920s. NPS rangers continue to operate the gate at West Yellowstone. As well as counting cars and visitors, they patrol the west boundary and maintain trails in the area. The uniforms have changed little since the 1920s, and as always, the rangers are the people who greet the world's visitors to Yellowstone.

This unique 1925 photograph shows Native American chiefs and tribal members from the Bannock/Shoshone Reservation near Blackfoot, Idaho, as well as the elaborate gate built at the west entrance. How long this gate was used is unknown. Legend held that Native Americans seldom came to the Yellowstone region. Today history gives evidence that as many as 25 tribes used the Yellowstone Plateau extensively.

In 1925, the governor of Wyoming, Nellie Ross (center with flowers), traveled to West Yellowstone for opening-day ceremonies. Until 1971, Yellowstone National Park was open during the summer months only. Opening day was usually June 20. The park closed on approximately September 15. Photographed to the left of Ross is Horace Albright, superintendent of Yellowstone Park, who staged lavish opening-day productions from 1925 to 1928.

Once at the gate, the tribal members danced and held ceremonies for the occasion. Dressed in their finest, Native Americans were part of all these opening-day ceremonies. The attendance of the National Park Service mounted color guard makes a statement of the importance of the park's opening for another year.

At the entrance are, from left to right, governors John Edward Erickson, Montana; Charles C. Moore, Idaho; George Henry Dern, Utah; and Nellie Taylor Ross, Wyoming, accompanied by park superintendent Horace Albright. The attendance of these dignitaries shows the importance of the park as it opened for another season. Tourism as a boost to the West's economy was early recognized.

Here the governors remove their respective gate logs to signify opening Yellowstone National Park for another season. Native Americans, National Park Service rangers, and throngs of visitors show what Yellowstone National Park had come to mean to people. Since its creation as a park in 1872, it remains one of the world's most cherished destinations. These early celebrations show that Yellowstone National Park was a fantastic place and wonderful to visit.

In this 1928 photograph, only two governors are present (in front of the table), George Henry Dern of Utah and H. Clarence Baldridge of Idaho. Also present were Supt. Horace Albright and dignitaries from the Union Pacific Railroad. This would be the last such celebration to be held at West Yellowstone. In the present era, the arrival of the first train is commemorated by the celebration of "Train Day" each June 11.

Eight

WINTER

It is another cold morning in West Yellowstone according to this 1953 photograph. Here Mildred Bartlett and her son, Arthur, bundled up for the cold, pose for a winter picture, perhaps to send to Mildred's family in Los Angeles, California. Such cold mornings are not uncommon in West Yellowstone, where the temperatures can reach as much as 55 degrees below!

In this early photograph from the Eagle collection, the family is preparing for a ski outing. Skiing, snowshoeing, and dog sledding were favorite pastimes during the long winters. Kids learned quickly to use "Norwegian Snowshoes," as skis were known then. Hills on the South Plateau and along the Madison River provided good terrain for such activities.

Cpl. Will Sager, facing the camera, and others soldiers, posted at the nearby Riverside Soldier Station sometime previous to 1916, are seen here in a winter camp. Note the long skis in the snow on the right; they could be as much as 14 feet long. These soldiers patrolled the west boundary of Yellowstone, looking for poachers and keeping a count of animals they saw.

In this c. 1940 photograph, the accumulation of snow covers the road and buildings. Only narrow lanes were kept open for traffic. Most of the businesses were closed, and the population was sparse. Those who stayed spent their time at school functions and playing grocery poker. It was a long wait until spring and the beginning of another year.

The Union Pacific dining lodge is snowed in for the winter. Operations here were shut down by mid-September. Although the roof on the south side, shown here, is usually kept clear of snow by the wind, the north exposures of the buildings accumulate a huge snow load that must be removed. This provided some welcome winter wages for locals.

Winter makes a special wonderland. A bit of that wonderland shows deep untracked snow that was the norm for years in West Yellowstone. Today the roads are maintained for over-the-snow vehicle use following the official opening of the winter season; that season was started in 1971. This additional season accounts for approximately 10 percent of the annual visitors to the area.

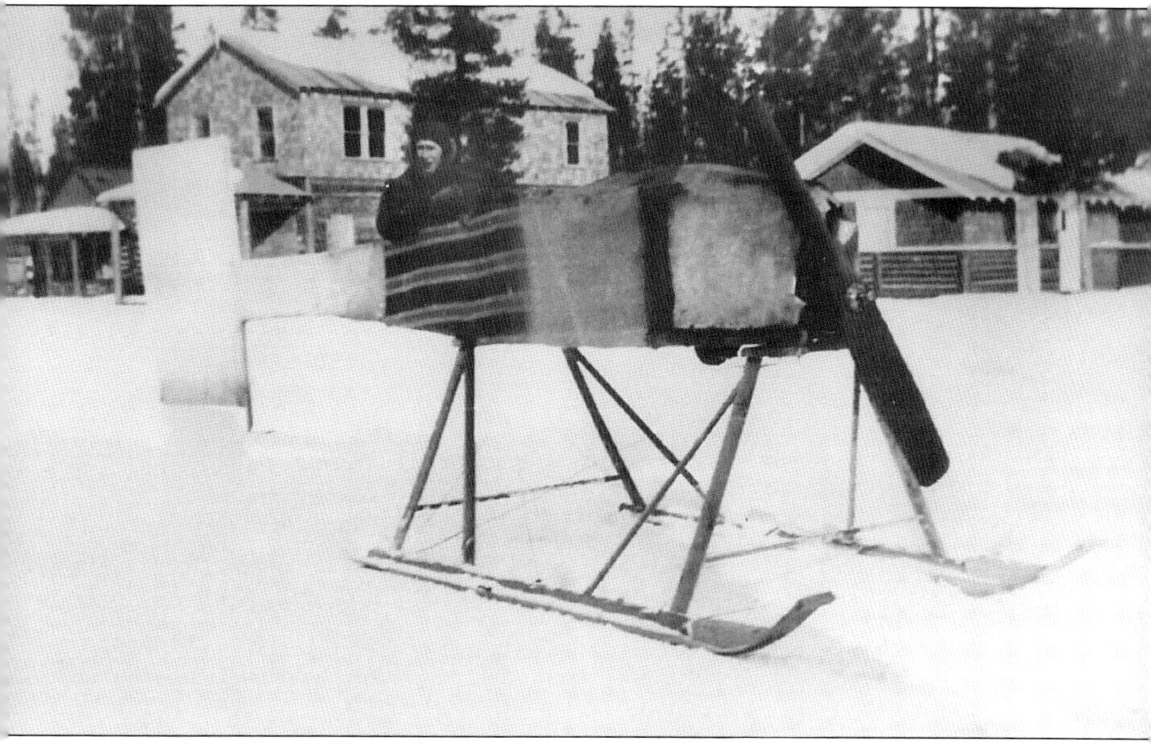

This undated photograph shows a brave soul in a homemade snow plane. It did not leave the ground, but it would have been a cold ride without a windshield. Such over-the-snow vehicles were a common backyard mechanic's toy in the long winter months found in West Yellowstone. This machine actually ran and must have provided for a lot of thrills.

Woodrow Bartlett, shown here with his 1940s snow plane, demonstrates the change from sleds and skis to motorized winter travel. Pushed by a small airplane engine, these machines were an innovation of local entrepreneurs, more a backyard mechanic's toy than a public conveyance. No brakes and awkward steering meant that they were used mostly on the frozen lakes nearby. By the mid- to late 1950s, several two-seat machines were taking visitors into Yellowstone National Park.

Clarence Bartlett is shown here with the same machine in front of Alex Stuart's garage. The Bartlett family had been in West Yellowstone since its beginning. Woodrow Bartlett's father owned Doc's Bar; Doc's younger brother, Clarence, was a mechanic and motel owner; and his older brother, Roxy, drove stagecoaches and built the Madison Hotel. These over-the-snow vehicles would be replaced in the early 1960s with small snowmobiles that could be operated by all.

In an undated photograph taken near Old Faithful, Walt Stuart and Lee Jacobson pilot their snow planes past Castle Geyser. The scene is a far cry from the crowds of snowmobilers that would be seen in Yellowstone National Park in the 1990s. The winter isolation of West Yellowstone was coming to an end; Yellowstone National Park would officially allow over-the-snow vehicles into the park in 1971.

Lion Head Ski Area opened near Targhee Pass in 1948. Here skiers wait to take the lift to the top. Skiing had always been a popular sport, and the townspeople decided to make use of the available natural terrain. They hoped that sufficient skiing traffic would make the train a practical answer year-round. Maintenance of the road to the lift and too few skiers made this a false hope.

The latest in ski lifts takes a skier up while another heads down. The Lion Head Ski Area was located on the west side of the basin and afforded views of the frozen Hebgen Lake and the Yellowstone Plateau to the east. With not enough business, the ski area eventual shut down. The lifts and buildings were removed and the area reclaimed into the surrounding forest.

Winter did not stop pilot Chris Christensen from freighting milk to town, as shown in this undated photograph. His airplane had skis attached to the wheels for landings and takeoffs. This risky venture once caused his plane to flip over, an event that covered him with broken eggs meant for delivery to West Yellowstone. Today's airlines serve only summer traffic.

Lined up in front of the Eagle Store, spectators watch the start of the West Yellowstone to Ashton, Idaho, Dog Sled Race in the mid-1950s. This race traversed 57 miles between the two cities and was one of America's premier dog sled races. This sport was seen in and around West Yellowstone in the early years. These sleds were one of the only ways to get around on unplowed roads.

This photograph shows John Hansen, husband of postmaster Alice Hansen, in front of one of West Yellowstone's early post offices. Deep snow did not stop the town's citizens from getting around. Before the roads were plowed, trails radiated from the school and were kept open by schoolchildren walking to and from home. One of the trails went into the Hansens' back door and out the front!

Here a deep cut through the snow has been plowed by the arriving "Spring Campaign" snowplow of the Union Pacific. The Spring Campaign marked the beginning of another season and the end of winter. On Reas Pass, it is not uncommon to measure 14 to 20 feet of snow accumulation during the long winter found in these parts. The line from Idaho was the only one that the Union Pacific Railroad allowed to be snowed in.

In this amazing photograph, railroad workers cut through steep banks in front of a steam- driven snowplow. Crews also dug out sidings and switches that were not accessible to the snowplows. Following a light winter, the crew could make it to West Yellowstone in one day, unless pushed off the tracks by the snow, which may be the case here.

A snowplow makes its way across Reas Pass during the annual Spring Campaign. The track from Ashton, Idaho, to West Yellowstone, Montana, was the only route on the Union Pacific Railroad that the line allowed to be snowed in. The railcar seen here is 14 feet tall, an indication of the snowfall in the high Rocky Mountains.

This photograph shows a forward view of a Union Pacific rotary snowplow crossing the divide between Idaho and Montana. A work train accompanied the plow with crews who would dig out the sidings, switches, and wye at West Yellowstone. After the arrival of this work train, the town traditionally held a dance and party for the crews to celebrate the arrival of another season.

In this 1969 photograph, a modern diesel snowplow opens up the West Yellowstone line for another season. Although passenger service was discontinued after the 1960 summer season, Union Pacific continued to plow out the line, using those 57 miles as a testing ground for snowplow equipment. The Spring Campaign, as it was called, dated back to the first year of rail service in 1908. (Photograph by William Kratville.)

Here the plow has made it to West Yellowstone in 1969. Another successful Spring Campaign is coming to a close. Crews still had to dig out the sidings and one side of the 2-mile-long wye. Union Pacific officials, seen here in suits, always accompanied the Spring Campaign in a separate train as part of the rites of another spring opening. (Photograph by William Kratville.)

Here in a mid-1920 photograph, special guests of the Union Pacific Railroad have arrived on the Spring Campaign train. The woman on the left wearing a cap is Marian Fish, a movie star of the day. She was married to one of the Union Pacific managers, Charlie Brooks; it took special connections to ride the Spring Campaign.

Locals look on in this photograph of Marian Fish's entourage. Apparently they were filming some sort of documentary, and that could have been the reason for Marian's trip. What was filmed and for what purpose is unknown, though. A local photographer took this and other photographs of her visit.

Here Marian Fish and a friend are skiing past the depot as enraptured local kids look on. The Spring Campaign was one of the biggest highlights of the year in West Yellowstone. It marked the beginning of another season and the end of winter. The town shut down and a large party was held in the evening for the arriving railroad crews and Union Pacific officials from Omaha.

Showing off for the guests, local kids ski off the roof of the depot. Such stunts were common, as was jumping off the dining lodge chimney into the deep snow. But this was a practice in the years when snowfall was heavy and deep. In more recent years, a drought has stopped such fun.

Marian Fish and some friends are at the auto entrance station on the boundary of Yellowstone National Park. A *Denver Post* newspaper article of the day stated that the Fish party had secured permission from the National Park Service to ski into Yellowstone. Thus, they could claim they were the first tourists of the year.

Pictured in this mid-1950s photograph are Harold Young and Bill Nicholls's new Bombardier Snow Coaches on a trip into Yellowstone. Although the park was not officially open, Nicholls and Young had a permit from the National Park Service to conduct the first winter tours. Some of these early snow coaches are still in operation and can be seen in West Yellowstone and the park even now.

By the early 1960s, the new snowmobile made its appearance in and around Yellowstone National Park. Here Harold Young's family and friends enjoy a day out in the mountains. The snowmobile would become the mainstay of West Yellowstone's winter seasons, which began officially in 1971 when the park opened for winter over-the snow travel.

Here is Harold Young on Two-Top Trail in the early 1960s with two of the new snowmobiles. With the introduction of the snowmobile, anyone could enjoy this new winter sport. Unlike the snow coaches and early snow planes, visitors needed no special knowledge to ride the trails. Two-Top is one of the premier trails to ride among the 1,000 miles or so of trails found just outside of Yellowstone.

This tranquil photograph was taken of one of the new Bombardier snow coaches making its way along the Lewis River near the south boundary of Yellowstone National Park. These over-the-snow vehicles and snowmobiles brought to West Yellowstone a two-season economy that did not exist before 1971. The park was now open during a season that had been closed for years.

Bibliography

Austin, Bruce, Robert Goss, and Gerard Pesman. *Buses in Yellowstone National Park.* Paramus, NJ: Motor Bus Society, Motor Coach Today, April–June 2000.

Dunbar, Jan. *It Is All True, or It Ought to Be . . . West Yellowstone Remembered.* Middletown Springs, VT: P.S., A Press, 2002.

Eagle, Ed, and Sam Eagle. *West Yellowstone's 70th Anniversary 1908–1978.* West Yellowstone, MT: Eagle Company, Inc., 1978.

Goss, Robert. *Yellowstone, The Chronology of Wonderland.* Gardiner, MT: self-published, June 2005.

Haines, Aubrey L. *The Yellowstone Story.* Vols 1 and 2. Yellowstone National Park, WY: Yellowstone Library and Museum Association, 1977.

Waite, Thornton. *Yellowstone Branch of the Union Pacific, Route of the Yellowstone Special.* Idaho Falls, ID: Brueggenjohann/Reese and Thornton Waite, 1987.

———. *Yellowstone by Train, A History of Rail Travel to America's First National Park.* Missoula, MT: Pictorial Histories Publishing Company, Inc., 2006.

Whittlesey, Lee H. "Marshall's Hotel in the National Park." *Montana: The Magazine of Western History* 30 (Autumn 1980): 42–51.

———. "Music, Song, and Laughter: Yellowstone National Park's Fountain Hotel: 1891–1916." *Montana: The Magazine of Western History* 53 (Winter 2003): 22–35.

———. *Yellowstone Place Names.* Helena, MT: Montana Historical Society Press, 1988.

Zaitlin, Joyce. *Gilbert Stanley Underwood, His Rustic, Art Deco, and Federal Architecture.* Malibu, CA: Pangloss Press, 1989.

Other Sources:

Montana Historical Society Archives, Helena, MT
Union Pacific Railroad Archives, Council Bluff, IA, West Yellowstone Files
Yellowstone Historic Center Archives, West Yellowstone, MT
Yellowstone National Park Archives, Gardiner, MT

DISCOVER THOUSANDS OF LOCAL HISTORY BOOKS FEATURING MILLIONS OF VINTAGE IMAGES

Arcadia Publishing, the leading local history publisher in the United States, is committed to making history accessible and meaningful through publishing books that celebrate and preserve the heritage of America's people and places.

Find more books like this at
www.arcadiapublishing.com

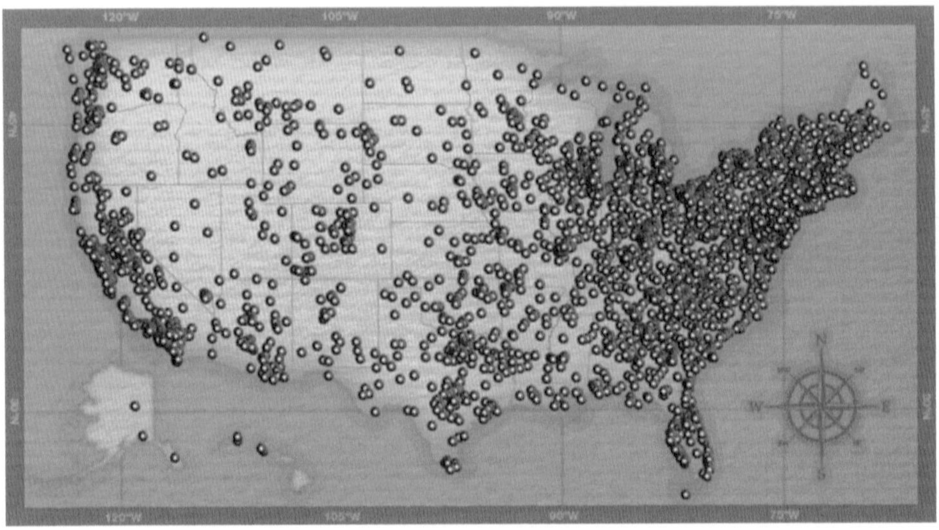

Search for your hometown history, your old stomping grounds, and even your favorite sports team.

Consistent with our mission to preserve history on a local level, this book was printed in South Carolina on American-made paper and manufactured entirely in the United States. Products carrying the accredited Forest Stewardship Council (FSC) label are printed on 100 percent FSC-certified paper.

MADE IN THE USA